Origami

Identifying Right Angles in Geometric Figures

Barbara M. Linde

PowerMath™

New York

Published in 2004 by The Rosen Publishing Group, Inc.
29 East 21st Street, New York, NY 10010

Book Design: Michael J. Flynn

Photo Credits: Cover, pp. 5 (all), 21 photos by Adriana Skura; p. 7 © Asian Art & Archaeology, Inc./Corbis;
pp. 9, 13, 17 photos by Cindy Reiman; p. 22 © Barbara M. Linde.

Linde, Barbara M.
  Origami : identifying right angles in geometric figures / Barbara M.
Linde.
       p. cm. — (PowerMath)
Includes index.
Summary: Explains the concept of right angles using the classic
folded-paper art of origami, and provides directions for making several
origami forms.
  ISBN 0-8239-8968-2 (lib. bdg.)
  ISBN 0-8239-8882-1 (pbk.)
  6-pack ISBN: 0-8239-7391-3
  1. Right angle—Juvenile literature. 2. Origami—Juvenile literature.
[1. Angle. 2. Geometry. 3. Origami.] I. Title. II. Series.
  QA482.L66 2004
  516'.15—dc21
                              2003002177

Manufactured in the United States of America

Contents

Origami and Right Angles

Origami is the art of paper folding. The word "origami" comes from 2 Japanese words. "*Oru*" means "to fold," and "*kami*" means "paper." When you fold paper, you create **angles** and shapes. If you know how to make angles and shapes with paper, you can make origami figures.

An angle is formed by 2 straight lines that start at the same point. Angles are measured in **units** called **degrees**. A right angle is an angle that measures 90 degrees, which is also written 90°. Two lines that form 1 or more right angles where they meet are **perpendicular** (puhr-puhn-DIH-kyuh-luhr) to each other.

Do you see any right angles in the origami figures on page 5? Right angles are often marked with a tiny square, like the right angles in this picture.

↗

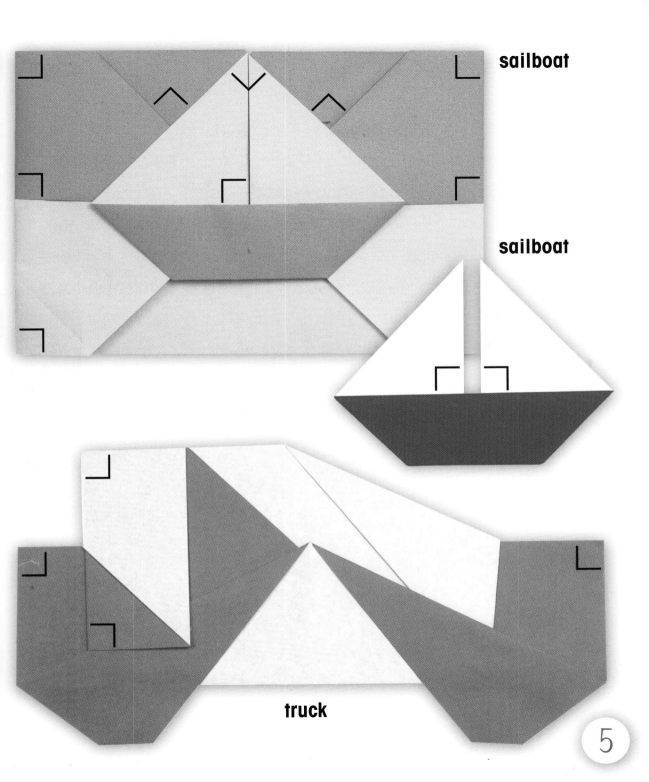

sailboat

sailboat

truck

5

The History of Origami

We are not sure where or when origami was invented. Paper was invented in China about 2,000 years ago. The art of paper folding may have started there around the same time. However, many historians believe the art of paper folding started in Japan. In the 600s, the Japanese learned about paper from the Chinese. The Japanese started to make origami figures of things they saw in nature.

Arabic **explorers** probably brought origami to the Arabic countries and to Europe. The Arabs studied the **geometric** shapes in the folded paper. Today, people all over the world do origami. In this book, you will learn to make origami shapes. Look for the right angles in the figures as you work.

The Japanese and the Arabs both used the art of paper folding to honor their religions. In fact, the Japanese word for paper, "*kami*," also means "spirit" or "god."

7

A Tower

This origami tower is made in **sections**. Each section is made with 8 square pieces of paper. The pictures on pages 8 and 9 show you how to make the folds.

1. Make 4 triangles by folding 4 pieces of paper from corner to corner. Do you see the right angle at the top of the triangle?

2. Fold each triangle in half, then unfold it halfway. Do you see the 2 right angles at the bottom on either side of the fold line?

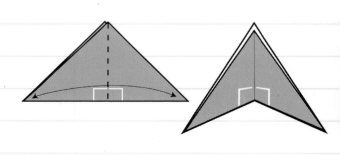

3. Make 4 rectangles by folding 4 pieces of paper in half. Each rectangle has 4 right angles.

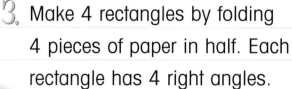

4. Fit each rectangle between 2 triangles to form a square shape. You have made 1 tower section!

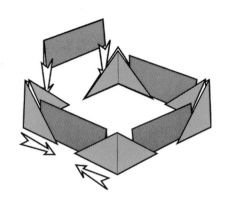

5. You can make more sections, turn them over, and stack them on top of each other. See how high you can build your tower.

Origami paper is square in shape. A square has 4 right angles and 4 equal sides.

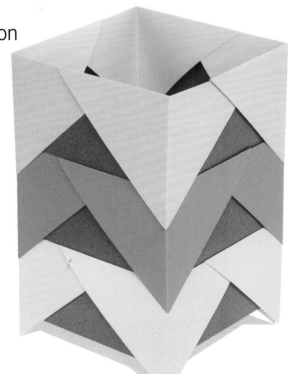

A Frog

You can make an origami frog that actually hops! Use a square piece of paper that is no larger than 6 inches by 6 inches. The pictures on pages 10, 11, and 12 show you how to make the folds.

1. Fold the paper in half to make a triangle.

2. Fold the left corner in to the middle of the bottom edge. Then fold the right corner in to meet the left corner at the bottom edge.

3. Turn the paper over so that the folded corners are turned away from you. Keep the folded parts at the bottom.

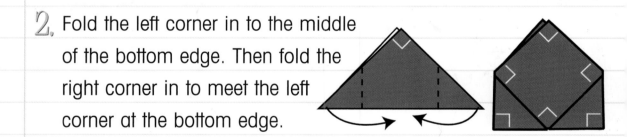

4. Fold the left edge to the middle, then fold the right edge to the middle.

How many right angles do you see after finishing step 4?
There are 10 right angles.

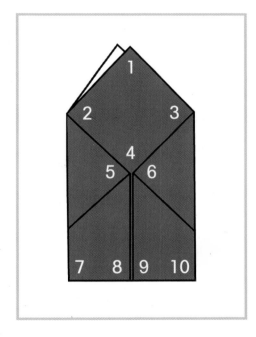

5. Unfold the 2 corners from the side of the paper that is turned away from you.

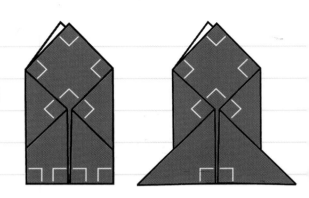

6. Fold the bottom edge of the shape up as shown in the drawing.

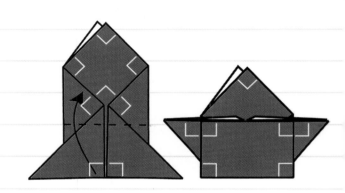

7. Now take the top edge of the part you just folded up and fold it down so it is even with the bottom edge. Turn the paper over. You have made an origami frog!

Once you have finished your frog, you can use it to play a game. Put your finger in the center of the bottom edge along the fold line. Press down quickly and remove your finger. The frog will jump! You and your friends can have a contest to see whose frog will jump the farthest.

Look at your finished origami frog and see how many right angles you can find. Don't forget to count right angles on the edges of the paper as well as right angles where the folded paper meets.

A Fish

For your next creation, you can make a fish. Use 2 squares of paper that are the same size. You can use 1 color for the fins and a different color for the body of the fish. The pictures on pages 14, 15, and 16 show you how to make the folds.

1. Fold the first square in half to form a triangle. Fold the second square in half, but then unfold it.

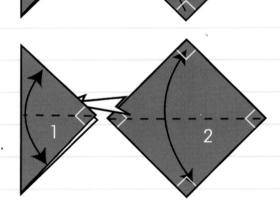

2. Fold the triangle in half, then unfold it. Slide the square between the layers of the triangle. The **creases** should line up.

3. With the square piece still between the 2 layers of the triangle, fold the 2 sheets in half.

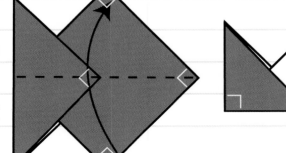

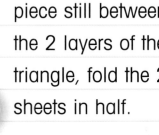

4. Fold the front pieces down along a line that goes from the center of the front angle to a spot about 1 inch above the right angle at the back of the figure.

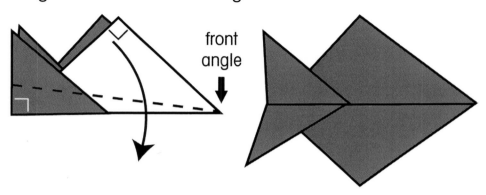

front
angle

When you use 2 pieces
of origami paper at the
same time, keep the papers
together. You will get sharp,
correct creases this way.

5. Fold the top edge of the paper down and behind the figure as shown in the drawing (fold A). Repeat this step with the bottom edge. Take the tips of the 2 parts you just folded behind the figure and fold them up to create fins (fold B).

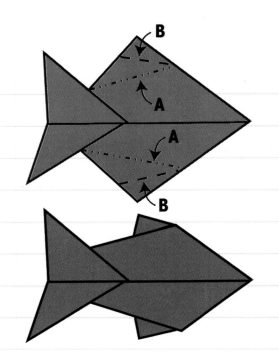

6. Fold the front tip of the fish back over the side facing you about an inch. This will make the fish's mouth.

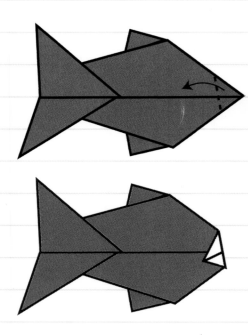

7. Make a fold on the top edge.
Make a fold on the bottom edge.
Now the fish has smooth sides.

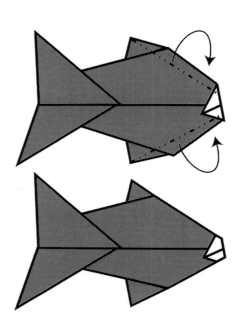

There are no right triangles in the fish at steps 5, 6, and 7. None of the lines meet at a 90° angle.

An Airplane

This airplane really flies! Use 2 squares of paper that are the same size. They should be no larger than 6 inches by 6 inches. The diagrams on pages 18, 19, and 20 show you how to do it.

1. Fold 1 piece of paper in half to form a rectangle. Now unfold the paper.

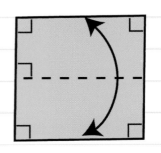

2. Fold the other piece of paper in half to form a triangle. Leave it folded. Fold the triangle in half from corner to corner, then unfold it.

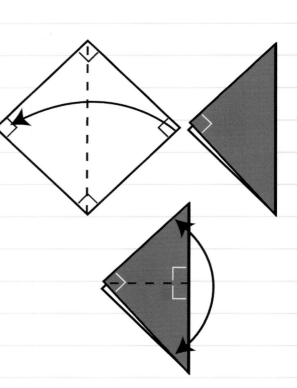

3. Slide the flat square between the 2 layers of the triangle. Line up the creases.

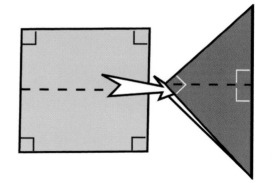

In step 1, the right angles are at the 4 corners of the square. In step 3, the right angles are at the corners of the square, on either side of the dotted line on the triangle, and at the left side of the triangle.

When you fold a square from edge to edge it forms a rectangle. The rectangle has 4 right angles. When you fold a square from corner to corner it forms a right triangle. The angle opposite the fold line is a right angle.

19

4. Fold up the long edge of the triangle. Make this fold where the edges of the 2 pieces of paper meet.

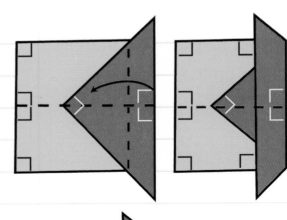

5. Fold the bottom edge up to meet the top edge. Now it is folded in half. Can you see the wings?

6. Fold the top edge of each side down to meet the bottom edge, then bring these sections back up until they stick straight out on both sides. This airplane does not look exactly like a real airplane, but it still flies. Try it out!

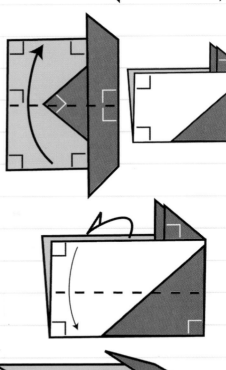

Make a plane with larger paper
and one with smaller paper.
Fly all 3 of them and see
which one flies best.

21

An Origami Crafter

Meghan Fureymoore has been doing origami for about 4 years. At first, Meghan followed the directions in origami books. Then she made her own origami creations. Last year Meghan created some Japanese dolls. She used pipe cleaners for the bodies and tissue paper for the heads. She made origami **kimonos** and hats. Meghan and her mom took the dolls to an art **museum** gift shop. Visitors bought all of them. Meghan is glad she knows about right angles and geometric shapes. This helps her with her origami creations.

Glossary

angle (AIN-guhl) A figure formed by two lines that start at the same point.

crease (KREES) A line or fold in paper.

degree (dih-GREE) A unit used to measure angles.

explorer (ek-SPLOR-uhr) A person who travels to new lands to find new things.

geometric (jee-uh-MEH-trik) Having to do with lines, angles, and shapes.

kimono (kuh-MOH-noh) A long, loose, traditional robe worn in Japan.

museum (myoo-ZEE-uhm) A building people can visit to see art or historical objects.

perpendicular (puhr-puhn-DIH-kyuh-luhr) A line that is at a right angle to another line.

section (SEK-shun) A part or piece.

unit (YOO-nuht) A standard amount by which things are measured.

Index